Free Things To Do on the

Las Vegas Strip

A Self-Guided Tour

By

Matt Lashley

Disclaimer

Although the author and publisher have made every effort to ensure that the information in this book was correct at press time, the author and publisher do not assume and hereby disclaim any liability to any party for any loss, damage, or disruption caused by errors or omissions, whether such errors or omissions result from negligence, accident, or any other cause.

Copyright © Matthew Lashley and Teela Books 2016

All photos courtesy of Rachel Osterman

All rights reserved

ISBN: 1533524084
ISBN-13: 978-1533524089

ACKNOWLEDGMENTS

I would like to give special thanks to my photographer Rachel Osterman for the images that accompany my text.

Table of Contents

Preface

Introduction

Our Starting Point - The Welcome to Fabulous Las Vegas Sign

Destination #2 - Mandalay Bay - Valley of the Falls

Destination #3 - Tram 1 Mandalay Bay - Luxor – Excalibur

Destination #4 - Hershey's Chocolate World – New York New York

Destination #5 - M&M's World

Destination #6 - Coca-Cola Store

Destination #7 - Tram 2 Park MGM to Bellagio

Destination #8 - Conservatory at the Bellagio

Destination #9 – The Water Show at the Bellagio

Destination #10 – The Wildlife Habitat – at the Flamingo

Destination #11 - The LINQ

Destination #12 – The Fall of Atlantis show – Caesar's Palace

Destination #13 – The Volcano show – Mirage

Destination #14 - Tram 3 Mirage to Treasure Island

Destination #15 - Photo op at Wynn water falls

Destination #16 - Circus show - Circus Circus

Destination #16B – Adventuredome

Destination #17 - The Viva Vision show- Fremont Experience

Destination #18 - Container Park

Appendix – The bus system for Las Vegas Blvd.

Preface

The Strip is world famous and not only for the casinos, but also for the many things to see and do. Of course, a lot of what you can do here costs money, but there are a number of things to do that are free.

This book is a self-guided tour, taking you step by step down the Strip to visit all of the notable free things to do. This excludes most of the photo opportunities, because the entire length of the strip is filled with places to take a photo of you, your friends and relatives. Only a few places of interest, directly in our travel path, are mentioned. Also, shopping sites have been excluded except for three unique stores of interest on the Strip.

The trip begins at the Welcome to Fabulous Las Vegas sign and ends in the downtown portion of Las Vegas Blvd. This is the old section of Las Vegas and is not considered a part of the Strip. I have included it to provide a complete Las Vegas experience.

Although the total distances for a complete trip are too long to experience on foot, most of the trip can be done without any cost in transportation by using the free trams. Only the last three destinations will require spending money on transportation, but a simple bus pass will suffice. The last two destinations are in downtown Las Vegas. However, instructions on how and where to catch the city bus are included. There is a special appendix on the bus system that serves the Las Vegas Strip. If you have a car, you can still visit all of these sites; however, where you decide to park is up to you. This tour guide is designed for a low budget, so worst case, you only need a 24 hour bus pass to complete the entire trip.

People arrive in Las Vegas with a certain limit to their spending, and even if a large portion of this is aimed at gambling, it is seldom possible to gamble the entire time you are here. If you need to take some time away from the slot machines, table games or sports book, you can visit a few of the destinations in this guide. The places I describe cost nothing, and will provide some getaway time for you and your friends or relatives.

With this in mind, I have written this publication about the points of interest that can be enjoyed for free along the Strip as well as a couple of spots in downtown Las Vegas.

Instead of simply listing the things to do for free, I have written them in chronological order, and provided instructions on how to get from one place to another. This has been done in succession, so you can travel a continuous path, moving from one point of interest to another.

Matt Lashley

Free Things To Do on the Las Vegas Strip: A Self-Guided Tour

Introduction

Although people can debate where the Strip ends, the consensus is that it begins with the Welcome to Fabulous Las Vegas sign, or if you want to reference a hotel, the Strip begins at the Mandalay Bay. It is generally thought of the south end of the strip being the beginning. I think this has to do with the large number of people coming from California on Intestate 15. Whatever the case may be, we will begin our journey from the southern end of the Strip.

A quick note before we begin. Almost the entire trip can be made on foot. Of course every person's ability to get around by foot varies, I'm in my fifties and walking is my primary form of exercise. I typically walk about 1.5 miles a day, six days a week. With the exception of the last three stops on the tour, I am able to complete the entire trip on foot. Naturally, you don't have to visit every stop on the tour, nor do you have to do it on foot. This is simply the vehicle I have chosen to tell the tale of a sight seeing trip of free things to do along the Strip.

Our Starting Point

The Welcome to Fabulous Las Vegas Sign

Our tour will begin at the Welcome to Fabulous Las Vegas sign. If you get here by car, you can only enter the parking areas from the southbound lanes on Las Vegas Blvd. If you are arriving by bus, the SDX will stop here (see appendix for bus instructions). It is also possible to walk here from the Mandalay Bay hotel, but only if you can handle a distance of one mile. I can walk it in about 25 minutes. There is a sidewalk for pedestrians that extends from the corner of the Mandalay Bay hotel to the Las Vegas sign; however, the heat in the summer time is too much for most people, and on some days in the spring, winter and fall, the wind can be irritating. If you are on foot, I recommend starting this tour by arriving by bus. You will be able to use your bus pass for the final two destinations on the tour as well as a return to the Strip, if that is where you are staying. The appendix in the back of the book explains everything you need to know to ride the bus on the Strip.

The Las Vegas greeting sign is world famous and needs no explanation. It has been here since 1959 and is a popular spot for getting a picture. In fact, it has become so popular that in recent years, it has gone through a special upgrade to accommodate both cars and people. It is no longer located on a wide, gravel divider, but it has been upgraded to include a small parking lot for cars, and a fence area where people can enter, taking turns photographing their friends and relatives. This has made the process orderly, so there is no longer a free-for-all to stand in front of the sign.

There are crosswalks on both sides of the median greeting sign area with signal lights to make it safe for pedestrians. Entering and exiting for cars is easy. These improvements have enhanced the safety of taking photos in front of the sign. This is much different than in the past when it was a bit of an adventure in getting that quick photo. In hindsight, it may not have even been legal, but today, it is not only legal, but highly encouraged. The only downside is that there is now a bit of a line to stand in front of the sign.

There are also bus stops and crosswalks on both sides of the street, so you can access the Las Vegas greeting sign by bus.

Getting to our Next Destination

After our visit to the Welcome to Fabulous Las Vegas sign, we will cross over the street on the opposite side we arrived on, and catch the bus back to Mandalay Bay. Use the crosswalk, but please be patient. The cars can move fast. Many of these cars are people arriving in Las Vegas just itching to make their first bet. Although it is only a short distance to cross the street (two lanes), wait for the green light.

After you catch the bus, you will be getting off at the next stop. This will be Mandalay Bay Road. After getting off the bus, walk back to Mandalay Bay Road and cross on the green walk sign.

Wait for the next green light and cross Las Vegas Blvd. You have now arrived at destination #2.

Destination #2

Mandalay Bay - Valley of the Falls

On the corner of Las Vegas Boulevard and Mandalay Bay Road (this is the street leading to the front of the Mandalay Bay hotel) is the entrance to what I refer to as the temple ruins. I am not certain exactly what it is suppose to be; it is referred to as the Valley of the Falls by the hotel, but it always reminds me of the ruins of an ancient temple in south east Asia.

This is the entrance from the street corner.

There is lots of vegetation, and once inside, it seems as if you are isolated from the outside world. Walk up the cement bridge until you reach the center of the structure. This is sort of a large gazebo area. On both sides you can see waterfalls, and there are also a few odd artifacts such as a large water barrel.

If you look high, toward the direction of the hotel, you can see carved elephants.

It's a quiet spot, except for the sound of the waterfalls, and also a good place to get a few good photos.

Here is a photo of a rope bridge, It reminds me of Indiana Jones.

I should point out that when the weather is nice, this area is closed to the public, because it is reserved for weddings. However, most of the times that I have gone there, it has been open.

After we are finished contemplating life and our existence in the temple ruins, we will proceed forward. The opposite way we came in. Our goal is to find the tram and take a trip north to the Excalibur.

Getting to our Next Destination

From the ruins, we will continue walking forward toward the hotel; this is the opposite direction we arrived from. Simply follow the cement walkway, past the waterfalls, and you will reach a tunnel. Walk through the tunnel.

When you have reached the other side, you will see a crosswalk. Look both ways and cross. Be careful, the cars can appear seemingly from nowhere in this area. Once you reach the other side, walk to your left on the sidewalk. There may be a sign pointing to the left. A few yards down the sidewalk, you will see the casino entrance to your right.

Once you are inside, you will see a sign that reads "escalator to resort and casino; follow the sign. Take the escalators to the next floor. Once you reach the top, turn right and walk until you reach a store, then turn left. Keep walking forward until you reach the casino floor, then turn right again. There will be a several stores to your right as you continue forward. Ahead, there will be a sign, and in the distance an escalator. You will be taking this escalator up to the next floor. You have arrived at destination #3.

Destination #3

Tram 1

Mandalay Bay - Luxor – Excalibur

This is the first of three trams that run along the west side of the Strip. All of them are free and serve to connect casino properties on the west side of the Strip, most of which are owned by MGM Resorts. These trams can be used as free transportation, but they are also something to experience for free on the Strip. The first time you go on the tram, you may want to go during the day, because you will be able to see more. However, you should think about traveling at night as well. With all of the lights, it can be pretty at night, but you may not know what you are looking at if you're seeing it for the first time.

This first tram I refer to as Tram 1, but I only do so because our tour is moving from south to north, and this tram is first one we will use.

There are actually two trams that you can catch here. Both of these trams travel from from Mandalay Bay to Excalibur; however, one of the trams will stop at the Luxor, while the other tram is non-stop from Mandalay Bay to Excalibur. Since we are traveling to Excalibur, either tram can be taken, but if you take the tram that stops at the Luxor, remember to stay on the tram. We will be getting off at the Excalibur stop.

Free Things To Do on the Las Vegas Strip: A Self-Guided Tour

The first time I took this tram, it moved a bit faster than I anticipated. It may have been because this tram operates out in the open, and it is easy to see the ground below. In fact, it is the only tram among the three that is easy to see from Las Vegas Blvd., at least during the daytime. If you do ride it during the day, the outside of the Luxor building and the statues below the tram tracks are eye catching, but there is nothing notable to do for free in this casino. Once the tram stops at the Excalibur, we will depart, and head to our next destination

Getting to our Next Destination

Once off the tram, follow the exit sign; you will go down a small flight of stairs. Make a right and head to the Excalibur; however, at the end of the bridge, you will make a right turn and walk to the pedestrian bridge that crosses over Tropicana Blvd. On the other side of the overhead crossing, take the escalator down to the street level, and walk around the Statue of Liberty. Take the escalator up and make a left, then walk through the entrance doors of New York New York. To your immediate right will be the entrance to Hershey's Chocolate World.

Destination #4

Hershey's Chocolate World – New York New York

This is a fairly new addition to the New York New York hotel. I am writing this in December of 2015, and if memory serves, they opened this store in the summer of 2014. So it hasn't been open for very long. If it has been a while since you have visited Las Vegas, this may be new to you. It is impressive for those who love Hershey candies or just chocolate in general. There is a wide assortment of Hershey products that are hard to find or only sold exclusively at this store. Well worth a look around. No purchase required.

Seeing this store at night is one of the prettiest places on the strip. A friend of mine tried to capture this in a photo at dusk.

Getting to our Next Destination

After you are finished visiting this store, you need to go back to where you came from at the top of the escalator. Make sure you leave from the same door you came in from. There are two levels. You came into the store at the top level, so if you went downstairs, you need to go back up to the second level. Otherwise, if you leave from the ground level of the store, you will need to make your way back to the escalator and go up to the top.

You will now take the pedestrian bridge over the Strip to get to the other side. Go down the escalator to reach ground level and turn around. You will be walking away from Tropicana Blvd, and the Tropicana hotel.

You will now take a leisurely walk down the sidewalk of the Strip, passing two or three stores until you get to M&M's world.

Destination #5

M&M's World

As with Hershey's Chocolate World, this is not a free thing to do unless you count shopping without buying anything, but it is a unique store and is the second of three stores we will be visiting on the Strip.

This has always been my children's favorite candy, so they always love visiting here. And for those who love this candy too, you should know that it goes way beyond a place to buy M&M's. They offer a wide variety of products that are made for fans of M&M's candy. There are four stories filled with exiting things offered for sale. Things such as clothing, coffee mugs, key chains, and a host of items that make good souvenirs. There are also things of interest that are not for sale. One example is an M&M race car.

Naturally, they have candy for sale. One interesting aspect of the candy offered here is the variety of colors available. They go far beyond the basic colors found in packages at your local market. They can be purchased by weight, and are dispensed from extremely tall containers. Just seeing this is worth a peak inside the store.

I am a diabetic, but as I wrote in my book, *Type 2 Diabetes: From diagnosis to a new way of life*, I can occasional treat myself to a few M&Ms of the peanut variety. So I am still a fan of these popular candies, just as my kids are.

Getting to our Next Destination

After visiting M&M's World, you will continue down the Strip in the same direction until you get to the large Coca-Cola bottle. A few feet passed this, you will see the entrance to the Coca-Cola store.

Destination #6

Coca-Cola Store

This store is similar to what you will find at the M&M's store except with the theme of Coca-Cola products. Clothing, accessories, as well as a variety of common and unusual products market with Coca-Cola products names and logos can be found here. The gigantic Coca-Cola bottle, which is actually an elevator, is a bit of an icon on the Strip.

I'm still waiting to find a Coke Zero t-shirt in this place; it is my favorite soda pop. Most of the items here revolve around Coke and to a certain extent Diet Coke.

Getting to our Next Destination

After visiting this unique store, you will continue in the same direction for a few feet until you come to a small street called MGM Street. Cross here, then prepare yourself to cross over the Strip. Remember to wait for the green light. You may see many people attempting to cross on a red because others are doing it, but this is dangerous. Wait for the green. After crossing here, you will make an immediate right turn. Keep moving in the same direction. After walking a few yards, you will approach the front of Park MGM (formerly the Monte Carlo). This is the casino that has the second tram that will take us to the Bellagio hotel and our next destination.

Walk up the steps of the hotel, and enter on the right side. you will want to head to the back of the casino where the pool area is located. When you see the pool sign, you make a right and walk down the hallway. The hallway is long and will make several changes in direction as you move through it, but there are no choices along your path; you will not get lost, just follow the signs.

The passageway ends at an escalator. Go up the escalator. After you make it to the top, move to your left and you will see a sign above a set of doors that says, "Tram to Crystal Shops and Bellagio." Go through the doors. You are now outside the hotel. Look forward and to your right, you will see another escalator moving up. This leads to the tram platform.

Destination #7

Tram 2

Park MGM to Bellagio

Once you reach the top, you will find two boarding areas for the tram. They are exactly the same. There are two trams. Both of them go to the same destination. They have two trams so they can move more people, and the wait isn't as long, so you will be able to catch the next arriving tram.

They have an LED sign indicating when the next tram will arrive. It usually isn't a long wait.

Free Things To Do on the Las Vegas Strip: A Self-Guided Tour

Once you are on the tram, remember that there will be two stops; the first stop is the Shops at Crystals. Simply stay on the tram; it is the second stop at the Bellagio that you want.

Getting to our Next Destination

Once you get off the tram, follow the signs to take the escalator or elevator to the level below. You will then go through the glass doors and walk about 20 yards to an escalator that will take you down one level. Walk through the passageway, there will be shops and other places of interest along the way. You don't have to be concerned about getting lost; there is no way you can make a wrong turn. At the end of the path you will see the conservatory on your left. You can't miss it.

Destination #8

The Conservatory at the Bellagio

This is a great free attraction on the Strip. This large room has been created to resemble a conservatory that might exist on the property of a large estate. The decorations change several times a year.

Often, there are themes that relate to the changing seasons. Because it is designed to give the appearance of a conservatory, all of the decorations are made to look as if they were created from flowers and plants. There are usually animals portrayed in the exhibit. Sometimes this place can be very crowded, especially on a Saturday evening, so it can be difficult to take pictures and see everything. Just remember to be patient and polite when you bump into other guests, and you will enjoy yourself.

The following photos were taken at various times of the year. The first was during the beginning of the Chinese New Year. It was the daytime, so the lighting was good.

Another display with a Japanese theme

Free Things To Do on the Las Vegas Strip: A Self-Guided Tour

This photo shows an under the sea theme

One last photo taken around Christmas has a winter theme

Getting to our Next Destination

After you're through seeing the conservatory, you will exit towards the hotel lobby. This is to your right, relative to where you entered the conservatory; you can see it from inside the conservatory. On the opposite side of the lobby desk will be the entrance to the casino. You will want to enter the casino on the far right side. You want to walk along the right side of the wall. You will move past shops, bars and restaurants, but keep going until you reach the shopping area. This will be to your right. There will be a sign that says, "North Entrance via Bellagio Shops." This is your next path.

You will travel past all of these retail stores until you reach an escalator that will take you downstairs. Straight ahead will be a revolving door. Go through this door, and you will be outside on the Strip. To your right you will see a large body of water. This is where you can see a free water show.

Destination #9

The Water show at the Bellagio

This is one of the popular free attractions on the Strip. Under high pressure, large fountains of water shoot high into the sky, choreographed to various types of music.

Show times can vary, but they usually start in the afternoon, and the last show stars at midnight. At the time of this writing, the times were listed as follows:

Monday - Friday 3:00 p.m. - 8:00 p.m. show every 1/2 hour 8:00 p.m. - 12:00 a.m. show every 15 minutes

Saturdays & Holidays 12:00 p.m. - 8:00 p.m. show every 1/2 hour 8:00 p.m. - 12:00 a.m. show every 15 minutes

Sundays 11:00 a.m. - 7:00 p.m. show every 1/2 hour 7:00 p.m. - 12:00 a.m. show every 15 minutes

Getting to our Next Destination

After you see the water show, trace your steps back to the revolving doors at the Bellagio and go through them. Move your way back up the escalator. At the top, follow the signs that say, "Caesar's Palace." You will be walking across the pedestrian bridge that passes over Flamingo Road.

Once you have crossed over, take the escalator down, and then proceed to walk around the corner of the of the intersection of Flamingo Road and the Strip. You will see another escalator. Take this up, and using the pedestrian bridge, cross over the Strip towards the Cromwell. Once on the other side, you will take the escalator down. Turn around and head towards the Flamingo hotel. We will visit the Wildlife Habitat inside this hotel.

It can be a little tricky finding the Wildlife Habitat because you have to make it through the casino. At the first entrance to the casino, you will walk straight forward on the carpeted path. After a few yards, it will slant right; you will walk past the food court. Keep walking until you see an overhead sign that contains several destinations, such as a restaurant and the pool. It will also say, habitat. Make a left. Go down a small flight of stairs. You will see the Wildlife Habitat on your right. You can't miss it.

Destination #10

The Wildlife Habitat – Flamingo

You'll want to get to the habitat while there is still light outside. The animals are not active in the evening.

This place is a bit of an oasis in the desert.

There are several animals to see while you are here. Naturally, the flamingos are a great attraction for visitors.

But there are a variety of birds here and exotic fish too. The largest species of fish can be found in the water near the buffet windows.

A portion of this habitat contains a chapel that is used for marriage ceremonies. If there are no marriages scheduled, this portion of the habitat may be accessible to visitors. There is a path that will take you up to the chapel. There is not a lot to see near the chapel, but here is a small waterfall.

The Wildlife Habitat is a relaxing place on the Strip, and you should find many photo opportunities here as well.

Getting to our Next Destination

The LINQ can be accessed directly from the Flamingo. Simply leave the habitat the same door you entered, but instead of going back to the strip, you will make a right and walk past the buffet; this will be to your right. Walk straight towards the exit doors a few yards ahead. These doors exit the casino, and will place you in the LINQ, which has been built along the side of the Flamingo hotel.

Destination #11

The LINQ

If you haven't been to Las Vegas in a while, you may not be familiar with the LINQ. It is basically a long, cobblestone road, with various shops, restaurants, bars and entertainment venues lining each side of the road. Naturally, there are no vehicles permitted here; it is designed for pedestrians only. Nothing here is run of the mill, and even if you find nothing that entices you to spend money, you will enjoy the sights. It will cost you nothing to walk the LINQ.

Turning to your left and towards the Strip, you will see a tall obelisk like structure that displays digital messages.

Looking to your right, and at the very end of the road, is the High Roller. This is a gigantic Ferris wheel, only nothing like you have seen before. Although they do have something similar in London, at 550 feet in height, the High Roller is claimed to be the tallest Ferris wheel in the world.

The compartments are large and keep the passengers inside, protected from the elements. You can walk directly underneath the compartments of the High Roller and observe passengers boarding and departing.

Getting to our Next Destination

Make your way back to the Strip. Once you exit the LINQ, you will be crossing the Strip to your right. Be patient. Wait for the green walk sign.

Once you make it to the other side, you will turn right and head north. Walk down the sidewalk and past the statues.

There will be an entrance to the Forum Shops with a sign at the top that says Forums Shops Caesars. Go through the entrance door.

The Forum Shops is basically an indoor mall, but to get to your next destination, we will have to travel down the entire length of this mall.

Destination #12

The Fall of Atlantis – Caesar's

This used to be the talking statue show that featured what appeared to be Caesar drinking from a goblet, and he would be talking. But I could never understand what he was saying. This show has now been replaced with one called the Fall of Atlantis. I still can't understand what is being said, but there are two gods who are apparently siblings and they are battling over who will gain control over their world from the king. One is female and the other is male. One is ice and the other is fire.

This is ice...

This is fire...

Standing between and above them is the king...

Free Things To Do on the Las Vegas Strip: A Self-Guided Tour

Fire and Ice prepare for battle...

The finale...

The show consists of a lot of propane use and a portion of it seems to dance on the water. The show doesn't last too long, but it is entertaining.

Show times begin around noon and can be seen every hour at the top of the hour. You should get here at least ten minutes early, so you can get a good spot to see the show. Right along the rail is best, but it can be a little warm with all of the flames.

I should also mention that there is a large salt water aquarium on the other side of the Fall of Atlantis show. It is approximately 50,000 gallons and holds a variety of colorful and interesting fish that swim among the sunken ruins of Atlantis.

Getting to our Next Destination

Our next destination is right down the street from Caesar's Forum Shops. Make your way back to the Forum Shops entrance and turn left. We will be walking north.

When you see a traffic light, wait for the green and cross. This is the exit for cars leaving the Mirage. On the other side of the crosswalk, you will keep walking and notice a body of water to your left, in front of the Mirage hotel. There is a facade of rocks that is the volcano.

Destination #13

The Volcano show – Mirage

This is a popular show on the Strip. It only lasts a few minutes, but in the darkness, it looks pretty good. For the most part it is simply water with red lights to create a lava effect. This combined with a lot of propane fueled flames, and you get a good fake volcano. You should get here at least 15-20 minutes before the show to get a nice spot to view the show. You might want to arrive a little sooner in the summer as the crowds are larger. If this is your first time, the volcano is to the right of the body of water in front of the sidewalk that runs along Las Vegas Blvd.

At the time of this writing the Mirage Volcano eruption could be seen starting at 8 p.m. and 9 p.m. Sunday through Thursday with an additional show at 10 p.m. on Friday and Saturday; however, the schedules are subject to change and vary by season.

Getting to our Next Destination

We will now catch the third tram, but you will need to catch it at the Mirage hotel, so turn back and walk to the traffic light you crossed to get to the volcano. After crossing at the green light, walk up the sidewalk to the Mirage hotel. When you arrive at the front entrance, keep walking. Access to the tram is outside of the hotel. Stay on the sidewalk, and you will notice the tram station straight ahead.

Destination #14

Tram 3

The Mirage to Treasure Island

This is the third of three trams, and like the other two, is free to use. It is the shortest distance traveled by any of the three trams, only covering the distance between the Mirage and Treasure Island. Although the trip only takes a few seconds, there is some scenery, if you look towards the Strip. To me, the Mirage at night, with its lighting, gives it one of the most beautiful appearance of any hotel on the Strip.

Getting to our Next Destination

When you arrive at the Treasure Island station, you will need to make your way through the casino and to the pedestrian bridge that crosses over Spring Mountain Road. This is the street that runs between Treasure Island and the Fashion Show mall.

After leaving the tram, you will move through the station doors and turn right, walk to the escalator, then go down. Walk straight until you reach the casino; you will see a gift shop on your left side. Make a left and walk along the wall – past the buffet and a bar. You will see the race and sports book straight ahead, keep walking. As you approach the sports book, there will be an escalator to your left. Take the escalator up, and you will arrive at the pedestrian bridge.

After crossing the first bridge, walk around the corner and down the Strip heading north, you will see the escalator going up. This will give you access to the pedestrian bridge crossing the Strip to the Wynn hotel. Once you get the end, take a right turn. This path will take you to the waterfalls.

Destination #15

Photo op at Wynn water falls

Although there is not much to see here for free, there is a nice waterfall, along with the occasional duck in the water. The vegetation is plentiful and relaxing.

A favorite place for many tourists to take photos.

Getting to our Next Destination

After spending a few minutes here, you will walk back to the escalator and go down to the street. If you are on foot, your journey ends here. However, if you have a bus pass, the bus stop is only a few yards north. You will be catching the Deuce; do not get on the SDX. The Deuce is the double-decker bus and will take you to our next destination.

After getting on the bus, you will be getting off at Elvis Presley Blvd. We will be crossing the street at the corner (in the crosswalk, when the light is green). Once on the other side, we will walk to the left, and then up the sidewalk next to Slots-A-Fun until we get to the doors of Circus Circus

Once inside, we will be heading to the Midway. This is a place with a carnival like atmosphere that has a wide range of booths with games of skill and chance. Naturally, these games cost money, but we are interested in the free circus show.

Destination #16

Free circus show - Circus Circus

The shows on the Midway are free of charge. The shows are not long in duration, but some of them can be quite entertaining. There are a variety of acts performed throughout the day. There are jugglers, dancers, and trapeze artists.

One thing to keep in mind is that it can be difficult to see the show unless you are in the designated seating area. Get to the show at least 15 minutes before it starts, so you can get a seat.

Destination #16 Part 2

Adventuredome

While you are here at Circus Circus, you might want to visit the Adventuredome Theme Park. It is an indoor amusement park that occupies more than five acres of land. Although the rides cost money, you can enter free of charge and stroll through the dome and experience the excitement around you.

Getting there is easy. Simply leave the Midway using the long ramp. Turn left at the bottom of the ramp. Walk past the gaming tables and make a right at the cashier's cage. You will walk past a Krispy Kreme on your left, then the buffet on your right. The carpeted path will lead you to the left and you will see escalators. Take it up, and when you reach the top, make a right. The Adventuredome will be on your left side.

You may want to walk past the first entrance, because they seem to always stop people to take their picture. I find this delay to be inconvenient. At the second entrance, there are no photographs. You can walk right in. You can see the entire amusement park by following the outside perimeter of the park. You will travel a complete circle and arrive back where you started.

Free Things To Do on the Las Vegas Strip: A Self-Guided Tour

Getting to our Next Destination

You will want to exit the same way you entered Circus Circus. You will want to catch the Deuce going north. This is the same direction you arrived, so you will be getting back on the bus at the same stop you arrived at.

Once outside, you will walk past Slots-A-Fun, make a left and cross the Strip. The bus stop will be to your right. Once back on the Deuce, you will ride this bus until you reach the downtown area. Your stop, will also be the last stop for the Deuce. This is

Fremont and Fourth Street, and it is the location of our next-to-last destination.

Destination #17

The Viva Vision show- Fremont Experience

Fremont Street was sealed off to traffic years ago. Today, you can take a leisurely walk down the heart of old Las Vegas. The canopy that you see at the top of the street is a large video screen. It is 90 feet wide and more than 1,500 feet long. Formally called Viva Vision, visitors often call it the Fremont experience.

The video screens are composed of millions of LED lights that display a variety of images that are accompanied by high quality stereo sound.

The shows typically run six minutes and can be seen every hour after the sun goes down. In the summertime this is 8:00. For the latest show information you can view their calendar at http://vegasexperience.com/calendar/

Getting to our Next Destination

Our last destination is on seventh street. You will be walking there. Simply head east, this is past the SlotZilla Zip Line and across Las Vegas Blvd. After crossing Las Vegas Blvd (this is the equivalent of Fifth Street in the downtown area), you will want to stay on the right side of the street. You need only walk two more blocks, and you will arrive at Container Park.

Destination #18

Container Park

Container Park will be located on the right side of the street, only a few yards past seventh street. As we approach Container Park, you may notice a large praying mantis in the front. It is easy to see in the daytime, but not as apparent at night. However, it is spectacular at night as flames shoot out of the giant insect's antennas. Even in the daytime, this can be impressive, but at night it is amazing and worth the walk just to see it.

Free Things To Do on the Las Vegas Strip: A Self-Guided Tour

Once inside the park, you will immediately understand why the facility is called Container Park. All of the stores are built out of shipping containers. The type that is used for international shipments of goods on barges across oceans. There is an assortment of stores and restaurants here. Most of them are unusual, off-beat shops, and there is usually something of interest for everybody. There is also a playground for children.

The End of Our Tour

The tour is now over. I don't want to leave you at Container Park, so if you arrived by bus, it is easy to catch the Deuce to head back to the Strip. Keep in mind that you catch the bus at a different location than you got off at. You will be walking back in the direction you came from, but the bus will depart on Las Vegas Blvd and Fremont Street. Simply head back down Fremont Street, until you reach Las Vegas Blvd. Cross when the light is green. Make a right and walk only a few feet to the bus stop. The bus will arrive just a short distance from where you crossed. For a reference point, the bus stop is next to the Heart Attack Grill.

In all likelihood, you read through this book before actually attempting to travel to all 18 destinations, so keep in mind that you don't have to visit everything, nor do you have to visit by bus. At the very least, I hope this book will help you find a few things to do while in Las Vegas that will cost you nothing.

Here's wishing you a lot of fun on your next trip to Las Vegas, and I hope you have a great time.

Matt

Appendix

The City Bus on the Strip

Although there are many ways to get up and down the Strip, the RTC bus system is without question the simplest and the cheapest. The Regional Transportation Commission (RTC) operates an elaborate bus system that serves the entire valley. However, as a visitor to the Strip in Las Vegas, you need only concern yourself with the buses that operate there.

There are two buses that operate along the Strip: The Deuce and the SDX. These two buses are easy to tell apart. The Deuce is a double-decker bus. The SDX has only a single story to it, but it is twice as long. Although they both operate on the Strip, the SDX is an express bus and does not pick up and drop off passengers at every bus stop along the trip, so it moves up and down Las Vegas Blvd more quickly than the Deuce, but you do need to know where it will stop in order to take advantage of the express nature of this bus. Because this is Las Vegas, naturally, both buses operate 24/7.

Except for the early morning hours, both buses arrive approximately every 15 minutes, so there is seldom a long wait. The Deuce operates from the Mandalay Bay hotel on the south end of the Strip and travels all the way to downtown Las Vegas. The SDX route travels well past Mandalay Bay on the south end. It travels to the popular Towns Square and to the Premium Outlets South before ending its southern trek at the Sunset terminal. Here, it begins its journey north.

The SDX travels north on the Strip until it reaches Desert Inn, and then it makes a right turn and heads to Paradise. It does this for those going to the Convention Center and Westgate hotel. The SDX doesn't get back to the Strip until the Stratosphere Hotel, so from Desert Inn to before the Stratosphere, visitors need to take the Deuce. The most popular destination it will bypass is Circus Circus. Also, the path the SDX takes downtown has an extended range from that of the Deuce. Although it will get you to the downtown hotel and casino area, it also loops around to the west and will take you to the Smith Center and the Premium Outlets North.

You can access more information about the two bus routes from the RTC website guide at this link: https://www.rtcsnv.com/wp-content/uploads/routes/2014/09/SDX.pdf

It costs $6 for a two hour pass; however, a 24 hour pass is only $8 and a good value. Passes can be purchased on the bus or at the vending machines located at most of the bus stops along the Strip.

Further information on fares can be found here:

http://www.rtcsnv.com/transit/fare-information/

I have taken the bus on the Strip at all hours of the day and week. For the most part, it isn't much different than any other city bus, but there are a couple of things to keep in mind. Because this is Las Vegas, the bus can become a bit rowdy, often with a party-like atmosphere. Sometimes people may appear to be intoxicated. Take all of this in stride. As long as there is no violence, remember to be tolerant. Also, these buses can become crowded, usually though, this is on the weekends or holidays. You may have to stand up, but younger people may give you their seat if you are an older person. If you find the bus too crowded, you can simply get off and catch the next bus.

About The Author

Matt is a writer and indie publisher who lives in Las Vegas, Nevada. Since his diagnosis of type 2 diabetes and subsequent success at getting it under control, he has written a book about his experience with the disease, *Type 2 Diabetes: From diagnosis to a new way of life*, and hopes that others can be helped with what he as learned about life as a type 2 diabetic. Matt currently is focused on writing about tourism in Las Vegas, Nevada.

Other Publications from Teela Books

Free Things To Do on the Las Vegas Strip A Self-Guided Tour By Matt Lashley

This book is a self-guided tour, taking you step by step down the Strip to visit all of the notable free things to see and do.

The Ultimate Guide to Free Things To Do in Las Vegas by Matt Lashley

This book is the ultimate guide to experiencing everything that Las Vegas has to offer that will cost you nothing.

22 Things to Do on the Las Vegas Strip for $25 and Under by Matt Lashley

The Las Vegas Strip is expensive! This books shows you all of the best tings to do for under $25.

How to Eat on the Las Vegas Strip for $10 or Less by Matt Lashley

Las Vegas doesn't want you to eat for under $10, but I have made it my mission to go up and down the Strip looking for the few possibilities that still exist.

Things To Do In Downtown Las Vegas by Matt Lashley

Read this book, and begin planning your next trip to Vegas to include Downtown Las Vegas.

Things To Do in Las Vegas Off the Strip – Away from the Neon Lights by Matt Lashley

Most of these places are not too far from the Strip and can be easily reached by car.

Shopping in Las Vegas by Matt Lashley

Learn where the best places to shop are when visiting Las Vegas.

The Best Free Photo Ops on the Las Vegas Strip by Matt Lashley

This book describes and shows photos of all of the best places to see and take pictures of, and all of these photo opportunities cost you nothing.

19 Valuable Horse Racing Betting Systems by Ken Osterman

These are methods and angles that have been among Ken Osterman's favorites over the years.

14 Easy-To-Understand Harness Racing Betting Angles by Ken Osterman

Learn how to compute several rating methods, along with easy spot play angles.

Betting Systems for all Major Sports by Ken Osterman

This book contains systems and angles for all four of the major sports in the United States. Professional football, basketball, hockey and baseball are all covered.

The Best Sports and Horse Racing Betting Systems That Work! by Ken Osterman

This book contains the best sports and horse racing betting systems from Ken Osterman previously published in two separate books: *Sports and Horse Racing Betting Systems That Work!* and *More Sports and Horse Racing Betting Systems That Work!*

The Quick and Dirty NFL Football Handicapping Method By Ken Osterman

This method will help you find an overlay in the point spread using the simplest and quickest method possible.

How to Handicap NFL Football The Smart Way by Ken Osterman

This book contains the entire book *The Quick and Dirty NFL Football Handicapping Method*. It also contains supplemental information to improve your handicapping, along with several spot play angles.

How I Made a 13.2% Profit Betting the 2018 College Football Season with a Simple Method by Ken Osterman

This is a powerful, mechanical method for handicapping college football games.

Betting on Major League Baseball

The Underdog Method By Ken Osterman

An easy-to-understand method that creates a money line that is used to decide if an underdog is a good wager.

Sports and Horse Racing Betting Systems That Work! by Ken Osterman

The book contains some of the best sports betting systems from Ken Osterman.

More Sports and Horse Racing Betting Systems That Work! By Ken Osterman

This is a sequel to Ken Osterman's *Sports and Horse Racing Betting Systems That Work!*. As with Ken's first book, there are methods for handicapping both horse races and sports.

The Path to Harness Racing Handicapping Profits by Douglas Masters

This book represents three decades of handicapping and betting harness races and is a summary of observations that are important to being a winning player.

Pure Speed Handicapping Quarter Horse Racing by Douglas Masters

Masters explains exactly how to create accurate speed ratings to give you an advantage over the rest of the betting public.

How to Handicap Quarter Horse Racing by Anthony T. Richards

Out of print for over 30 years, this fascinating book on handicapping quarter horse racing is now available again.

Stealth Betting Systems for Winning at Casinos by Luke Meadows

Author and casino gambler, Luke Meadows, explains his betting methods he uses in Las Vegas casinos in an easy-to-understand way.

Type 2 Diabetes: From diagnosis to a new way of life by Matthew Lashley

This book tells the story of how my diabetic condition was discovered, my denial of the condition, then the work done to get my glucose level to levels that are close to normal.

The Dream is Gone Economic Survival in 21st Century America Say No to Credit – Say No to Banks by Ron Charleston

Economic survival means breaking free from a system that takes from you and offers nothing in return. The only solution is to break free from it.

Make Money Online Without Spending Any Money By Ron Charleston

Teaches you to make money on the internet at home, from your computer, without spending a dime.

The Grim Truth About Bitcoin

by Ron Charleston

This book cuts through all of the propaganda that is espoused and promulgated by the devotees of that which is called Bitcoin.

Memoirs of a Life of Confusion

by Matt Lashley

A light read about events that have confused me in childhood, family meals, school, religion, reality, language, parenting, and as an adult. I hope it will bring a smile to your face.

Free and Low Cost Online Promotional Techniques for Self-publishers of Kindle and POD Paperbacks by Matt Lashley

This book will teach you all of the best free and low-cost promotional techniques for your books, and all of it can be done right from your computer.

For the latest information about our publications, along with articles by some of our authors, please

visit our website.

http://www.teela-books.com

Matt Lashley's YouTube channel *Stuck in Vegas*

Teela Books Publishing YouTube channel *Teela Books*

Teela Books Publishing Bitchute Channel *Stuck in Vegas*

Made in the USA
Monee, IL
12 January 2023

25163853R00056